THE SELECT NONSENSE OF SUKUMAR RAY

Translated by
SUKANTA CHAUDHURI

With an Introduction by
SATYAJIT RAY

OXFORD
UNIVERSITY PRESS

OXFORD
UNIVERSITY PRESS

Oxford University Press is a department of the University of Oxford.
It furthers the University's objective of excellence in research, scholarship,
and education by publishing worldwide. Oxford is a registered trademark of
Oxford University Press in the UK and in certain other countries

Published in India by
Oxford University Press
22 Workspace, 2nd Floor, 1/22 Asaf Ali Road, New Delhi 110002, India

First published in 1987
Oxford India Paperbacks 1997
31th impression 2022

ISBN-13: 978-0-19-563039-8
ISBN-10: 0-19-563039-4

Printed in India by Manipal Technologies Limited, Manipal

For SIDDHARTHA

INTRODUCTION

My father died when I was two and a half. Hence I never had the opportunity to know him as one comes to know one's relations. I know him instead through his writings and illustrations, a volume of drafts, some notebooks, two numbers of a hand-written magazine, and the accounts of my mother and other members of the family.

Sukumar Ray was born in 1887. His mother Bidhumukhi Debi was the daughter of Dwarkanath Gangopadhyay, that brilliant and spirited member of the Brahmo Samaj. Sukumar's father was Upendrakishore Ray, whose many-sided genius found expression in his writings, songs and illustrations as well as his work as a printer. We find in Upendrakishore a rare combination of science and the arts, the east and the west. He played the pakhwaj as well as the violin; wrote devotional songs while carrying out research in printing methods; viewed the stars through a telescope from his own rooftop; wrote old legends and folktales anew for children in his inimitably lucid and graceful style, and illustrated them in oils, water-colours and pen-and-ink, using truly European techniques. His skill and versatility as an illustrator remain unmatched by any Indian.

Sukumar grew up under the influence of such a father. He was the second of six children, three brothers and three sisters, the eldest being Sukhalata. He was educated at Calcutta. His only known juvenilia are two pieces in the magazine *Mukul*, set up by Shibnath Shastri.

Soon after leaving college, Sukumar founded the Nonsense Club with his friends and relations as members. Its name indicates the direction that his genius was to take. He wrote two plays for the Club, *Jhalapala* (Cacophany) and *Lakshmaner Shaktishel* (Lakshman and the Wonder Weapon) and ran a magazine, *Sarey-Batrish Bhaja* (Savoury Mix). These contain the first expressions of Sukumar's humour. Of the two plays, the second is the better, although the first does not lack touches of originality. Characters out of the *Ramayana* descend in *Lakshmaner Shaktishel* from the epic heights to a world of spoof and horseplay. Unpoetic matters easily find place here : vegetable curry, Bathgate the chemists, homoeopathic drugs, Sandow the muscleman, recurring decimals. Hanuman the monkey-god eats sugar-puffs, the Messenger of Death finds his salary in arrears. Of the other monkey-heroes, Sugrib wraps a bandage round his foot while Jambuban is annoyed by the stink of Bibhisan's beard. Sukumar also makes his debut here as a composer of songs. His simple tunes and rhythms add greatly to the fun.

But neither play contains any hint of the distinctive vein of humour in which Sukumar is unrivalled. This we first glimpse in the magazine *Sandesh*.

In 1911, five years after graduating with double Honours in Physics and Chemistry, Sukumar went to England for advanced training in printing technology. The next year, Rabindranath Tagore arrived in London with the manuscript of his English *Gitanjali*. Upendrakishore was Tagore's friend and coeval, and Sukumar one of his band of young admirers. Englishmen were as yet unacquainted with Tagore's genius. Sukumar helped to pave the way by reading a paper on 'The Spirit of Rabindranath' before the Quest Society.

The children's monthly *Sandesh* was launched in May 1913 with Upendra-kishore as editor. Sukumar returned home a few months later, and his writings and pictures began to appear in *Sandesh*. There were relatively few in the first three years, as Upendrakishore was alive and amply furnished the pages with his own work. His writings and illustrations, especially the latter, bear proof that he too was a fine humorist, with a simple, tender humour utterly free of satire or irony. Those who knew him affirm that his humour was a reflection of his personality.

Sukumar's humour too was free of malice, but not of satire. At times he could indulge in a frank roar of laughter, and this again agreed with his particular personality. Many people have told me of his fun-loving, outgoing nature and his brilliant conversation.

Neither Upendrakishore nor Sukumar had any formal training in art. No one would guess this from the quality of Upendrakishore's work, but it is perceptible in Sukumar's. In sheer drawing skill, Sukumar is not his father's equal; but he makes up for this by two rare gifts, a remarkably observant eye and a limitless fund of imagination. Through a union of these two qualities, his subjects transcend all criteria of technique and acquire living form before our eyes. That is why we cannot doubt the existence of any creature he portrays, real or imaginary. Chandidas's Uncle or the Old Man of the Woods, the Griffonling or the Higgle-Piggle-Dee — all are equally alive, equally credible.

Sukumar's special literary bent appears already in some contributions to *Sandesh* during his father's lifetime. In 1914 appeared 'Khichuri' (Hotch-Potch), the first of the *Rhymes without Reason* (*Abol-Tabol*). Here we find the earliest nonsense animals in Sukumar's work, born out of games with language :

> A pochard and a porcupine, defying the grammarians,
> Combined to form a porcochard, unmindful of their variance.

Similar whimsical compounds create the Storkoise, the Whalephant, the Parakizard, the Liontelope. Not content with naming them, he also drew their likenesses for our benefit.

Within a few months, readers of *Sandesh* were introduced to the Old Man of the Woods. This timber technologist belongs to a class of characters of whom Sukumar was especially fond. There is no lack of pedants and eccentrics in this world, with their eyes turned towards a land of their own grotesque imagination. Sukumar permits them to realise their dreams. 'The sky's full of soot, so the wood runs to holes.' The proponent of so startling a theory might be scorned by society, but he will surely find a welcome in the poet's world. Alongside him we must place Chandidas's Uncle, the Shadow-Catcher, the Baboo with the moustache and the inventor of the Penetroscope.

Such characters are not always human beings; sometimes they appear as imaginary animals. The first to arrive was the Lug-Headed Loon, who thinks and feels like a human but looks like a zoological medley. There had been imaginary animals in old Bengali nursery rhymes, but they lacked character and personality. Closer to Sukumar's are the weird creations of Lewis Carroll or Edward Lear. Carroll's 'Jabberwocky' reminds us somewhat of Sukumar; but there is a basic difference. The creatures in 'Jabberwocky' belong to such a remote world of the imagination that they need utterly new words to describe them :

> 'Twas brillig and the slithy toves
> Did gyre and gimble in the wabe.
> All mimsy were the borogoves,
> And the mome raths outgrabe.

Lear, too, created many nonsense animals : the Dong, the Jumblies, the Pobble, the Quangle-Wangle, the Blue Boss-Woss. But these again are not allowed to come too close to our familiar world. Their realm is virtually that of the fairy tale.

The Lug-Headed Loon, on the contrary, lives in Bengal; and further,

> The Inspector of Drugs   Is an uncle of Lug's,
> He has no other living relation.

In the same way, the Blighty Cow can readily be seen in Haru's office; the Super-Beast 'wails on the meadows and weeps by the streams'; and the Pumpkin-Puff seems to prowl around our houses, otherwise we need not have been so mindful of his wishes. Only the Griffonling lives in isolation for obvious reasons, but even then not in fairyland. It is not quite the real world either, needless to say. It is a world all Sukumar's own, and its creation is his finest achievement.

Although Upendrakishore saw the first products of his son's genius, he did not live to follow its full course. He died in 1915 at the age of fifty-two; and the editorship of *Sandesh* naturally passed to Sukumar.

At this point of time was born the Monday Club, or the 'Candy Club' (*Manda Sammelan*) as Sukumar called it. He was the leading spirit of this group, which included some of the most promising young artists, writers, critics and scholars of the day. Apart from Sukumar and his brother Subinay, there were the poets

Satyendranath Datta and Ajit Kumar Chakrabarti; Suniti Kumar Chattopadhyay the philologist; Atulprasad Sen, poet and composer; Kalidas Nag, scholar and litterateur; Prasanta Chandra Mahalanabis the statistician; Prabhat Chandra Gangopadhyay the Bramho leader; Charu Chandra Bandyopadhyay, scholar and writer; and Nirmal Kumar Siddhanta the educationist. The transactions of the club covered diverse matters from Plato and Nietzsche to Bankimchandra and Vivekananda, the poetry of Tagore and of the Vaishnav poets. There were also musical sessions, dinners, picnics and general merrymaking. The notices were printed at Sukumar's press, and their language too was distinctively Sukumar's. Once while the secretary was absent, the members received a printed postcard whose message might be expressed as follows :

> The Secretary, curse his face,
> Has simply sunk without a trace.
> And now we see, alack! alack!
> The Club descend to ruin and rack.
> So Monday next, to hold our meet,
> To Garpar, to my humble seat,
> Your venerable steps address
> And help the Club to clear its mess.
> And bring along a book or screed
> From which you feel you'd like to read.
> ____ Thus begs, with lowly namaskar,
> Your faithful servant, Sukumar.

Besides the Club, Sukumar had another field of activity that needs mention. This was connected with the Brahmo Samaj. One of the chief purposes of Sukumar's life was to form an association of youths to revive Brahmo ideals and practices through weekly lectures and discussions. The proud history of the early Samaj inspired him; he seems to have been depressed in equal measure by certain contemporary lapses from that ideal. One detects a note of disillusionment in his late work, *Atiter Chhabi* (Pictures from the Past), a versified history of the Brahmo Samaj for children. Nowhere else in his writings do we find such a note.

Of Sukumar's writings for adults, composed before he took charge of *Sandesh*, one might mention certain essays on art and language in the journal *Prabasi*, and the two plays *Chalachittachanchari* and *Shabdakalpadruma*, which we may inadequately render as 'The Busy Bee' and 'The World of Words'. The essays reveal Sukumar's incisive modern outlook. The plays are chiefly vehicles for ideas; even their conflicts are conflicts of ideas. But their chief attraction lies in the sparkling comic dialogue. These two plays are the finest examples of the sociable, conversational genius of Sukumar that I described earlier. Hence they are best staged in informal, intimate surroundings.

Sukumar's writings for children grew day by day after he assumed charge of *Sandesh*. Its pages were crammed not only with stories and poems but also with attractive essays, news from all over the world, folk-tales from home and abroad, novel puzzles and riddles. One may derive certain lasting principles of good children's literature from any issue of *Sandesh* of this date. There had been school stories earlier in Bengali; but it was for Sukumar to demonstrate in *Pagla Dashu* (Daft Dashu) how such stories ought to be written. It is futile to look for sentimental moralising in *Pagla Dashu*. We should read it instead to find out how to bait the teacher with fire-crackers.

A few months after Sukumar became editor, there appeared a short story in *Sandesh* which I would place among his masterpieces. It has the nonsense-title of *Drighangchu*, and describes the reaction to a crow's sudden entry into a royal court and its solemn intonation of the syllable 'Caw'. At the end, the king has to stand before a crow on the palace roof and repeat a four-line chant or spell. A ten-line version of this rhyme is used by Sukumar as the chant of Viswakarma in the play *Shabdakalpadruma*. It goes something like this :

A green and gold orang-outang,
Rocks and stones that jolt and bang,
A smelly skunk and izzy tizzy,
No admission, very busy.
Ghost and ghoul, do re mi fa
And half a loaf is better far.
Coughs and colds and peanut plants,
Pussies are the tiger's aunts,
Trouble-shooters, blotted blobs,
City centre vacant jobs.

It would be hard to find a better example of the pure spirit of nonsense. We can scarcely tell where its success lies, why the least change in an arbitrary sequence of references would impair the effect. It can be neither analysed nor imitated, and only sheer genius can produce it.

Sukumar named this special vein of nonsense the *rasa* or spirit of whimsy. Needless to say, it is not one of the nine *rasas* of Indian dramatic theory. There are traces of such whimsy in the folk poetry of any nation. But authentic literary nonsense masks its caprice beneath an apparent gravity in an urbane and sophisticated manner unknown in popular rhyme.

There has been wit and humour in Bengali literature, both poetry and prose, from the earliest times; but there is little or no nonsense. This is not to say that Sukumar derives nothing from his predecessors. He uses puns, alliteration and onomatopoeia for humorous effect just as others had done earlier. But the special quality of his nonsense is largely his own creation. If we are to talk of influence, we must think not only of the Bengali tradition but also of European literature, the pantomime, Charlie Chaplin and western comics. (As Sukumar's illustration makes clear, the candle-sucking brats in 'Infant Joy' were inspired by the Katzenjammer

Kids of the American comic strip.) Sukumar had his doubts as to how the Bengali reader would react to this vein of nonsense. The preface to *Abol-Tabol* carried an apologia : 'This book was conceived in the spirit of whimsy. It is not meant for those who do not enjoy that spirit.' We may recall that Tagore too had to provide such a defence for *Khapchhara*, the book of nonsense verse that he wrote in his old age.

Sukumar edited *Sandesh* from 1915 to 1923, chiefly from his sickbed for the last two and a half years. Yet one is amazed at the extent and excellence of his work. He devoted much labour not only to writing and drawing but to devising new printing techniques. A notebook of this time lists some of the processes he invented. He had planned to take out patents for them, but did not live to do so.

As far as his writing and drawing go, nearly all his best work belongs to these two and a half years. *Ha-Ja-Ba-Ra-La* (*A Topsy-Turvy Tale*) was written in 1922. The finest piece of nonsense in Bengali prose, the *Tale* is obviously influenced by *Alice in Wonderland.* There is the same falling asleep on the grass; the same dream; the same pageant of known and half-known beasts and humans; the same hits at linguistic lapses, social customs and legal procedures; and finally the return to reality. Yet nothing could be more quintessentially Bengali than the latent spirit of this topsy-turvy world.

Heshoram Hushiarer Diary belongs to the same period. This too is nonsense, but in a spirit of parody. the object being Conan Doyle's story about Professor Challenger, *The Lost World.* In Sukumar's tale, Challenger becomes Professor Hushiar, and the setting is an unknown part of the Karakoram Mountains. We have a profusion of prehistoric animals not to be found in the textbooks. Only Sukumar knows about them, and only he could have named them, in matchless compounds of Latin and Bengali. He has also drawn them so convincingly that we feel quite shocked not to find their fossils in the museum.

Again and again during his illness, Sukumar returned to a particular poetic project of which fragments are scattered through his notebooks. He named it *Sri Sri Barnamalatatva* (Holy Alphabetology). It would have provided an exciting climax to the traditional alliterative techniques of Bengali poetry. Sadly, Sukumar did not live to complete the work.

None of Sukumar Ray's writings appeared in book form in his lifetime. *Abol-Tabol* was published on the 19th September 1923, nine days after his death. Although he did not see the finished book, he had designed from his sick-bed the cover in three colours, the lay-out, some short rhymes as space-fillers and the illustrations for the tail-pieces. His last composition was the final poem of *Abol-Tabol* (here entitled 'Dream Song'), whose mingled strain of fancy and humour must remain an object of wonder in Bengali letters. The last few lines indicate how he was living in the shadow of death :

A keen primordial lunar chill,
The nightmare's nest with bunchy frill —
My drowsy brain such glimpses steep,
And all my singing ends in sleep.

I do not know of any other humorist who could jest in this spirit at the meeting-point of life and death.

*　　　*

Sukanta Chaudhuri asked me to write an introduction to his admirable translation of some of my father's nonsense verse and prose. I had already written a foreword in Bengali to a collected edition of my father's works, and it was later decided that Sukanta himself would translate this foreword and make it serve as an introduction to his book. The above is the result of his effort. Some passages which proved untranslatable have been left out. I had also made the remark that it was impossible to imagine *Ha-Ja-Ba-Ra-La* being translated into any other language. This too has been left out because Sukanta's very able and imaginative translation of this Carrollian fantasy is a refutation of my contention.

SATYAJIT RAY

TRANSLATOR'S PREFACE

Clever men might debate whether nonsense can be translated; but I reassure myself that at worst, the result will still be nonsense. All the same, I have left out eight poems from *Rhymes without Reason* and a few short passages from *A Topsy-Turvy Tale*. The omissions either relate to untranslatable points of Bengali idiom, or else appear to lose all their fun in translation — at least in my translation.

In translating Sukumar Ray's verse, I have adhered as closely as possible to the original metres and rhyme-schemes. I should also point out that many of the English names exist in the original. I have introduced 'Brother Ned, and Brother Joe' in 'Glee Song', and another Joe in 'Burglar Alarm', not to mention Tom, Dick and Harry; but Uncle Tom in 'Infant Joy' and young Master Booth in 'The Gift of Tears' were so christened by Sukumar himself. The illustrations, needless to say, are Sukumar's own.

My warmest thanks to Mr. Satyajit Ray for his generous encouragement; more specifically, for letting me translate his Bengali introduction to his father's works, and for helping to name the Higgle-Piggle-Dee.

Contents

RHYMES WITHOUT REASON

A translation of *Abol Tabol*

HOTCH-POTCH

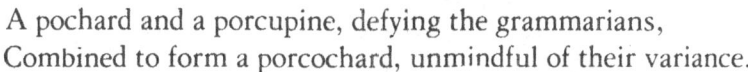

A pochard and a porcupine, defying the grammarians,
Combined to form a porcochard, unmindful of their variance.

A stork upon a tortoise grew, exclaiming 'What a hoot!
A very handsome storkoise, now, we jointly constitute.'

A parakeet its features lent unto the lowly lizard,
In puzzle whether flies or fruit would better suit its gizzard.

The very goat began to feel impatient of its state :
It leapt upon a scorpion's back, and grew incorporate.

The tall giraffe refused to roam its ancestral savannah,
But tried to don a locust's wings, and glide in graceful manner.

The cow was led to view itself, and staggered from the shock :
Its noble form had been usurped by some designing cock.

And rent by schizophrenia the whalephant we view :
The open seas, the forest trees are tearing it in two.

The lion longed for antlers, and was doomed to dwell in care
Until a stag supplied it with a truly splendid pair.

THE OLD MAN OF THE WOODS

A grumpy old man sat and humpily chewed
A stump of old timber, well shredded and stewed.
He muttered and hummed as he made his repast :
You'd think him a scholar, in quandaries cast.
His words were a riddle to ignorant souls :
'The sky's full of soot, so the wood runs to holes.'
He sat in the sun with a sweltering pate,
And grumbled, 'Who cares for these matters of weight?
I'm sick of these people, all doltish and blind.
To carping and wrangling unduly inclined,
Yet utterly dead to a scientist's goals,
On new-moon nights why the wood runs to holes.'
He puzzled and pored over intricate sums
Of wood that has crannies and wood that has crumbs,
Of cracks that are bitter and cracks that are sweet,
And cracks whose bouquet is an epicure's treat.
One log with another he stroked and he tapped,
Exclaiming, 'Now here's the whole picture I've mapped!
I've given my lifetime to stumps and to sticks,
The rascally timbers I fitly can fix,
I know which are peaceful and which rather wild,
The logs that are lusty and logs that are mild,
And logs with philosophy lodged in their souls —
The thousand-odd reasons why wood runs to holes.'

TICKLE-MY-RIBS

S. Ray.

You may roam round the world or go sailing in ships,
But keep right away from old Tickle-My-Ribs.
He's not worth a visit, the fearsome old bore :
He'll tickle you dead if you land at his door.
He creeps up from nowhere on poor passing blokes
And draws them apart, and starts telling them jokes.
God knows where he picks up each wearisome tale —
They leave you less minded to laugh than to wail.
No sound and no sense to them, reason or rhyme —
And yet he insists that you roar every time.
And not just content with this verbal attack,
He takes a long feather and tickles your back,
And chortles, 'It's killing — our Kestodas' aunt
Sold eggs, yams, and pumpkins, and linseed to plant.
The eggs were quite slender, the pumpkins were balls,
The yams were all painted with colourful scrawls.
And all day she warbled with dulcet report
"Mew-mew", "Gobble-gobble", "Woof", "Hee-haw" and "Snort".'
He pinches you black to induce you to chuckle,
And pokes at your ribs with a scrawny old knuckle
Or tickles your side as he tumbles with glee :
You must wring out a laugh if you want to go free.

THE PURLOINED MOUSTACHE

The Baboo at the Central Works seemed always mild and mellow.
How could we tell he'd prove to be a most aggressive fellow?
We'd left him very happily relaxing in his bureau,
When suddenly he broke out with a truly shocking furore.
He sat up with a vicious start and thrashed his limbs about,
And rolled his eyes, and cried, 'Be quick! I think I'm passing out.'
So some call for an ambulance, and some for the police,
And someone warns, 'He'll try to bite, so gently if you please.'
In midst of this, with thund'ring voice and features grim and swollen,
The Baboo roars, 'Confound you all! My whiskers have been stolen!'
A whisker-thief! How could it be? Who'd heard of such a snorter?
And there we saw the whiskers plain, not shrunk the least iota.
We told him so in clearest terms, and held up looking-glasses :
We'd never known a whisker come to such regretful passes.
At this he really hit the roof, and screamed to all the writers,
'I don't believe a word you say — I know you lying blighters.
This whisker's like a dirty broom, all bunched and coarse and scary :
I saw it once upon the lout that runs the local dairy.
I'll murder any slanderous rogue who dares to say it's mine.'
An so he took his ledger book and charged them all a fine.
Then puffed and choked with mortal rage, he penned a memorandum :
'The office staff are thick as planks, I simply cannot stand 'em.

4

You mustn't ever give 'em rope, be taciturn and harsh.
The pack of dolts have even failed to guard my prize moustache.
I wish that I could catch these chaps and tweak their mangy stubble,
Or chop their silly noddles off for causing all this trouble.
They think they own their facial hair — O road to all disasters!
It's whiskers, now, that make the man, and they're our lords and masters.'

*　　*　　*

A MARRIAGE IS ANNOUNCED

I went to Posta, and they said
Your daughter was about to wed,
And Gangaram's the lucky man!
So let me tell you what I can.
Dear Gangaram's a comely youth —
A shade too dark, to tell the truth —
And on his face, a constant scowl
A little like an angry owl.
His scholarly accreditations?
You must admire the young man's patience.
He tried full nineteen times to get
His Junior School Certificate.
On top of that, he's rather poor :
The wolf's for ever at their door.
His brothers are a precious lot,
For one's a freak and one's a sot,
And one assumed the noble mission
Of forging notes, and went to prison.
The youngest plays a set of drums
In music-halls for modest sums.
Poor Gangaram's for ever ailing
With jaundice and a kidney failing.
But still, they're of a noble breed :
The Grand Panjandrum's direct seed,
And Lahiri of Banagram
Is cousin, now, to Gangaram.
So now you've got it cut and dried —
A worthy match for such a bride!

5

THE POWER OF MUSIC

When summer comes, we hear the hums of Bhisma Lochan Sharma.
You catch his strain on hill and plain from Delhi down to Burma.
He sings as though he's staked his life, he sings as though he's hell-bent :
The people, dazed, retire amazed although they know it's well-meant.
They're trampled in the panic rout or languish pale and sickly,
And plead, 'My friend, we're near our end, Oh stop your singing quickly!'
The bullock-carts are overturned, and horses line the roadside;
But Bhisma Lochan, unconcerned, goes booming out his broadside.
The wretched brutes resent the blare the hour they hear it sounded,
They whine and stare with feet in air or wander quite confounded.
The fishes dive below the lake in frantic search for silence,
The very trees collapse and shake — you hear the crash a mile hence —
And in the sky the feathered fry turn turtle while they're winging.
Again we cry, 'We're going to die, oh *won't* you stop your singing?'
But Bhisma's soared beyond our reach, howe'er we plead and grumble :
The welkin weeps to hear his screech, and mighty mansions tumble.
But now there comes a billy goat, a most sagacious fellow,
He downs his horns and charges straight, with bellow answ'ring bellow.
The strains of song are tossed and whirled by blast of brutal violence,
And Bhisma Lochan grants the world the golden gift of silence.

* * *

Now did you hear what Sitanath has said he thought he fancied ?
It seems he's been to sniff the sky, and found it rather rancid.
Of course, the odour goes away if it should rain or sleet;
For then I've often had a lick and found it fresh and sweet.

THE INVENTOR

Chandidas's Uncle has devised a grand machine :
They've praised it in the highest terms wherever it's been seen.
Indeed, they say this Uncle, at the tender age of one,
Would burst out crying 'Goongaa' in a manner fit to stun.
Now 'Mama', 'Gaga' and the like are all that kids can babble,
So 'Goongaa' from this prodigy astounded all the rabble,
And learned men would prophesy, 'Now should this child survive,
We'll bet our beards he'll find a course to keep his name alive.'
That infant grown to riper years has worked a fine invention
To cover five hours' walk in one, without fatigue or tension.
I've been to see the contrivance — it's quickly understood.
Just handle it five hours or so, you'll get its hang for good.
But words can scarce describe the work the learned world has praised :
It's fixed upon your shoulder, with a rod in front upraised,
And there you hang the kind of food you find the most enticing —
A pie or pasty, fry or roll, or cake with almond icing.
The mind aspires to reach the food, the lips move forth to swallow,
The dainty flies before your gaze, and you perforce must follow.
Thus spurred along by gluttony, you walk without a heed :
The more you see the dangling bait, the more your turn of speed.
A score of miles you quickly stride and never tire the least,
With watering mouth and glinting eye agog to chase the feast.
So now you know why man or boy who views this exhibition
Returns amazed, and joins the ranks that hail the man of vision.

SHADOW PLAY

I tell you it's true, for I never invent —
I've wrestled with shadows until I'm quite spent.
A good many years have I followed this trade,
By sunlight or moonlight to capture each shade :
The soft morning shadows, all damp with the dew,
The hot frizzled shadows of mid-summer too.
When eagles and kites on their wanderings go,
Their swift roving shadows I trap down below.
I've sampled the shadows of crows and of crakes,
The damp cloudy shadows that drift on the lakes.
There're nobody knows this, or cares an old boot :
There's nobody skilled in this subtle pursuit.
The shadows of trees seem to utter no sound,
We think they lie peacefully sprawled on the ground —
But you'd be surprised if I told you the facts
Of what my research has revealed of their acts.
When everything's still, they will start from their sleep,
And nuzzle around as they wander and peep,

And that's when you cautiously creep up behind
And fling down a basket to keep them confined.
No leaf, root or bark has such sovereign might :
There are pale toothless shadows and ones with a bite,
And each one attacks its particular bugs :
Diseases run screaming at sight of such drugs.
The bitter-leaf shadow, extracting the core,
Induces sound sleep and a musical snore.
The papaw-tree shade by the moon I distil
To cure the catarrh and get rid of the chill.
The shadows of nut-trees discolour and crimp,
But grow a sound leg on a man with a limp.
Or if the damp weather you seek to survive,
The warm shade of tamarinds keeps you alive.
And now for a secret : I'm nursing the vapour
Of wild honey-berries on damp blotting-paper.
We'll soon have a nostrum, all home-made and new,
And just fourteen annas the price of the brew!

PUMPKIN-PUFF

If Pumpkin-Puff should dance —
Beware! Beware! You mustn't dare beyond the stalls advance.
You musn't glance to fore or aft, or cast your eyes aslant,
But grapple close with tips and toes the Rancid Radish Plant.

If Pumpkin-Puff should cry —
You simply musn't mount the roof to contemplate the sky.
But stretched upon a pumpkin-frame and muffled in a quilt,
Sing hymns to Radha-Krishna with a slily solemn lilt.

If Pumpkin-Puff should roar —
You perch upon a single leg beside the kitchen door;
Then whisper Persian verses with an eloquence forlorn,
And slink entirely supperless to lie upon the lawn.

If Pumpkin-Puff should run —
You scramble up the window-frame as though you'd heard a gun;
Your cheeks and chin anoint with care in talcum blent with tar,
And never turn your eyes aloft to gaze upon a star.

If Pumpkin-Puff should wail —
You're meant to don your legal hats and climb into a pail.
You make a paste of spinach-pulp to plaster round the nape,
And heat a piece of pumice-stone and give your nose a scrape.

Perhaps you scorn my warning words, or think they sound demented.
If Pumpkin-Puff should find you out, he'll make you sore repent it.
And then you'll see my prophecies fulfilled in every letter :
So don't blame me — it's you who thought you knew your courses better.

SAFETY FIRST

Pelaram Biswas, what's happened today?
What makes you breathe in that dangerous way?
Haven't you heard of poor Bhutanath's death?
Why, right to the end he kept drawing his breath.
Here are you gaping, your mouth all awry —
What if you happen to swallow a fly?
Old Hala Ray, in one of his rages,
Swallowed a fly and was laid up for ages.
That's why I'm telling you — do have a care,
Watch where you step, and for God's sake beware
Of looking right, left or behind as you go :
Fortune favours the cautious and slow.
Think of that fable where Thingumajig
Fell down a well-shaft, or some sort of rig.
And while we're about it, you'd be a fool
To go for a dip in the Ghoshes' old pool.
You're not quite as slim as you might be, what?
So why let happen what you'd rather not?

Now don't blow your top. You may win through, no doubt,
But if not, dear chap, you're the one to lose out.
For God's sake stop arguing — you make me wild,
Mister Know-All, and yet almost a child.
Well, do what you like, just ignore my advice,
But trust me, one day you'll be paying the price.
Ramesh's uncle, another such dolt,
Flouted my health tips in stupid revolt.
And what would you have? In the open bazaar
He pipped it, poor fellow, knocked down by a car.

O come and consider my surgical arts,
This snipping and slicing and joining of parts.
I think of the day that I heard from my master,
'Start off with patients of paper or plaster.'
Heart all a-glow with this counsel of vigour,
I stuck to my bench with the uttermost rigour,
My blood turned to ice with my labours unwearied —
But frankly, it isn't as hard as we fear it.
You tap and you tear — see the range of my tools?
And fix 'em again as you're taught in the schools.
It's fun to dissect all these lovely big dummies :
You just close your eyes and you slit up their tummies,
Or chop off a leg, or a shoulder or two,
Then patch up the bits with a quick dash of glue.
I've been through the drill and the examinations —
I think I should start on some real living patients!
A mere half-a-dozen would do to begin :
Old Nandy next door is as stubborn as sin,
He thinks he's arthritic, and just won't be cured :
I'd have him in straight if he'd only be lured.
Now who's got a sniffle, or ache in the ear?
You're saved, my good fellow! The doctor is here.
And bring that poor devil who's broken his leg —
It won't take a minute to drive in a peg.

You're puffy and swollen — a toothache I read :
A rap with a hammer is just what you need.
Both this jaw and that — why, you're shockingly toothed :
I'll just get my pincers and see that you're soothed.
The young and the aged, the blind and the lame,
The new case and chronic I treat just the same.
A fracture or fever, the gout or the glands —
They just need a touch of my versatile hands.

THE MIRACLE MAN

That doctor's amazing! They say the old sinner
Puts food in his mouth when he's eating his dinner,
And also feels hungry if starved of his bread,
And closes his eyes when he sleeps in his bed!
He walks with his feet always treading the ground,
His eyes can see things, and his ears can hear sound.
On his shoulders, they tell me, his head you can view :
O let's go and see if such things can be true!

13

SNAKES ALIVE

Baburam, snake-man,
Where do you make, man?
Stop for two shakes
And sell me some snakes.
They mustn't have claws,
Or nails, or jaws,
Not run nor fight,
Nor *ever* bite :
To lunge or hiss
Would be most remiss.
I'd keep them fed
On milk and bread.
If you get me a pair
Of serpents so rare,
With my cudgel bold
I'd soon knock them cold.

THE OWL'S LOVE SONG

Said the Owl to his mate, 'O my peach,
How sweet, I aver, is your screech!
Each squawk that your mandibles utter
Reduces my heart to a flutter,
The croaking crescendos you capture
Inspire me with fathomless rapture!
Your tremolo flows all a-quiver,
The trees grow ecstatic and shiver,
And O what an intricate tangle
Of titters you mix and you mangle!
All torment and trembling and sorrow,
Despond for the past and the morrow,
The pit-a-pat play of my tensions,
Are drowned by your dulcet inventions.
Such strains from your sweet pout leaping
Unman me with measureless weeping!'

BURGLAR ALARM

It's a scandal, I tell you — a standing disgrace,
Such roguery heedless of person or place!
In the hour before lunch, while I steal forty winks,
The size of my dinner-pack suddenly shrinks.
I'm plagued every day by this rascally thief,
But yesterday's damage surpassed all belief.
There were five nice cutlets, a large loaf of bread,
A mixed plate of sweets — a magnificent spread,
With French fries and salad and what have you got .
I wake up to find that he's cleared the whole lot!

I'm furious today — there are bounds to my patience.
I've had quite enough of these foul depradations.
So watch me stand guard, at alert all the day :
I'll see who can dare steal my dinner away.
Whether Tom, Dick or Harry, or Joe down the block,
I'll halt his designs with a little sharp shock.
I musn't be fooled by his shifts and devices,
But just grab his collar and carve him in slices.
I'm lying in ambush, with sword and with shield :
I'll wait till he enters, then force him to yield.
I've warned him enough, but he simply defies me.
I've got him today where he cannot surprise me.

ALL'S WELL

I've thought about this long and hard,
And find it rather funny —

I love all things material :
I love the fake, I love the real,
I love the poor and also pelf,
I others love and love myself,
I love the sound of tinkling bells,
I love the flowers and their smells,
I love the sky with cloudlets lined,
I love the merry tossing wind,
I love the sun, I love the rain,
I love the white, I love the stain,
I love the meat, I love the rice,
And fish with marrow's very nice :
I love the raw, I love the cook'd,
I love the straight, I love the crook'd,
I love the drum with cymbals match'd,
I love the bald head and the thatch'd,
I love to wheel a push-cart in,
I love to roll a rolling-pin,
I love to hear a raga sung,
Or see the bolls of cotton wrung,
I love to bathe in water cold,
But everything being said and told —

The thing I really most regard
Is eating bread and honey.

SUPER-BEAST

A very weird creature, of no proper breed,
Went grumbling all day out of envy and greed.
He wailed on the meadows and wept by the streams
With sulking demands and exorbitant dreams.
You scarcely could tell why he kept up his whine,
Forever complaining, 'I wish it were mine.'
He wanted a voice like the cuckoo's refrain;
So practised his crooning, but warbled in vain.
He envied the birds as they soared in the sky,.
And wished he had wings, and could learn how to fly.
With trunk and with tusk see the elephant tread :
So why should he settle for less on his head?
He viewed the lithe kangaroo bounding along,
And longed for his legs to be lanky and strong.
For the lion's proud mane he would also make suit,
The long scaly tail of the lizard to boot.
He called on all creatures to please all his whims,
And moaned to the world for his maladroit limbs.
When lo and behold! On the fifth of July
He suddenly gained all he'd wanted to try!
But once the excitement was utterly over,
He found that he wasn't quite living in clover.
Should elephants prance in such lolloping manner?
Or kangaroos feed off a stalk of banana?
If Squat-Head cried 'Cuckoo', would people be rapt?
Would an elephant's trunk on that torso be apt?
Supposing they jeered at a jumbo that flew,
Or tweaked his poor ears and guffawed and cried 'Boo'?
Supposing they challenged him, right to his face,
'You nameless old boob, you're a proper disgrace.'

He couldn't reply, for he'd have no defence,
So burst out at last in his anguish intense :
'I can't be a moth or a horse or a snake,
A bee or an elephant, donkey or drake,
A fish or a frog or a bird or a tree,
A shoe or a sunshade —
Oh what *can* I be?'

THE RULE OF TWENTY-ONE

In Lord Shiva's native land
The laws are hard to understand.
If you trip and come a cropper,
You're collared by the nearest copper,
The magistrates upon you seize,

And fine you twenty-one rupees.

You also need a special lease
Till six o'clock to cough or sneeze,
And those who sneeze without permission
Are thrashed in gentle admonition,

And twenty-one compelling doses
Of snuff rammed up their streaming noses.

On each loose tooth they charge a cess
Of four rupees, not more nor less;
And whiskers grown in sundry manners
Attract as toll a hundred annas —
They prod your back and twist your arms

To jerk out twenty-one salaams.

If strolling forth, you ever chance
To right or left to turn or glance,
They send a message to the King —
His scouts ride forth to haul you in,
And stand you in the mid-day sun
        To drink of cups full twenty-one.

There people who indulge in verses
Are caged up straight with muttered curses.
A hundred hinds, in varied rhythms,
Recite to them the logarithms.
They're made to check through grocers' tills
        And work out twenty-one long bills.

If in the middle of the night
You snore out loud and start a fright,
They rub your head with home-made cures
Of apple juice and farm manures.
        You make them twenty-one devoirs
        And get strung up as many hours.

*   *   *

It seems an awful pity,   In the Crooked Cranky City
    The doctors scorn to eat their rice with spuds.
They've published many papers   That tubers have their vapours
    Which spoil the brain, and wisdom never buds.

THE LUG-HEADED LOON

The Lug-Headed Loon   Sits sunk in gloom
     In his home in deepest Bengal.
Not a smile on his face —   Does he dwell in disgrace?
     Has anyone asked him at all?

The Inspector of Drugs   Is an uncle of Lug's,
     He has no other living relation.
Can that be the clue   To his pallor of hue
     As he sits there in dumb desolation?

O there was a time   When with song and with rhyme
     He stumped it in dance all the day.
You could hear from afar   His 'Trim-tra-la-la'
     As he shuffled his footsteps in play.

I sigh and recall   How he'd perch on the wall
     And gobble bananas with glee.
What could have transpired?   Has his uncle expired?
     Or could he have fractured his knee?

'There, that's quite enough,'   He cries in a huff,
    'Don't you know why my wits seem a-wander?
'I'm wrapt in surmise   On the swatting of flies,
    And the hours pass by as I ponder.

'If here to my right   A fly heaves in sight,
    Why then, with *this* tail I can fell him.
'Or if he should chance   From the left to advance,
    This other tail's handy to quell him.

'But what if he's sly   And chooses to fly
    Right here in the middle?' he wails.
'Oh how can I plug   The canny old bug?
    I haven't got more than two tails!'

*   *   *

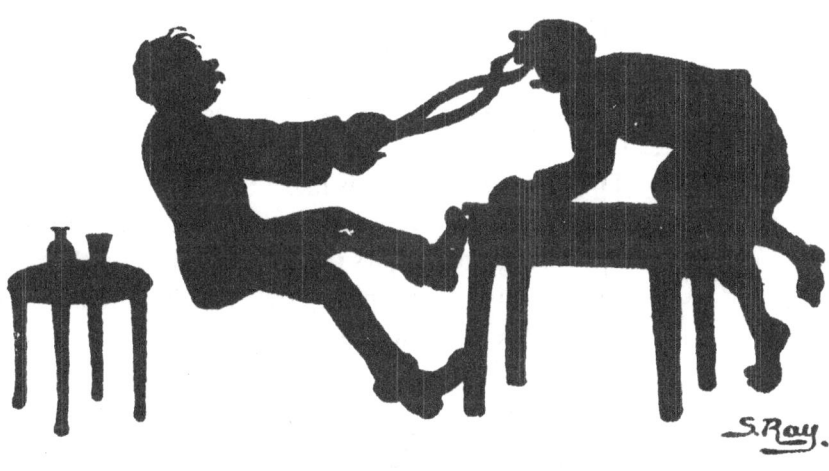

The rainbow spreads its glorious shades,
    And people crowd to watch it.
'Dear me, this colour quickly fades,'
    Cries old Carp, in a crotchet.

THE CUSTOMS OF BOMBAGARH

Have you heard of the monarch of Bombagarh's orders
To fry mango jelly and frame it with borders?
And why does his queen wear a pouffe on her head?
Or the queen's eldest brother knock nails into bread?
There people turn cartwheels to cure their catarrhs,
Rub rouge in their eyes by the light of the stars,
Musicians walk muffled in blankets of state,
And bald-headed scholars stick stamps on their pate.
But why should they pickle their watches in whey?
Or line the king's mattress with sandpaper grey?
The king sits and howls like a fox in the court,
On his lap the Chief Justice thumps pitchers for sport,
They hang broken jars from the throne and the walls,
And the king's aunt plays cricket with pumpkins for balls.
Her brother goes waltzing, with hookahs adorned.
But what does it mean? Could we please be informed?

THE MUSIC-MAKERS

The cars go up and cars go down, the streets are choked with traffic,
The people rush on every side, and jolt and press and maffick.
They rush around for bedlam bound, are hit by cars and scattered,
The sahibs stare and send up prayers as if the whole thing mattered.
But we will only strike the beat and sing our merry lay,
   Diddle-diddle-boom! Derray, derray, derray.

The monsoon rains have swept the town and filled the streets with mud ;
Why court a cramp from cold and damp or chill your precious blood?
It might be dawn, it might be dusk, it might be afternoon,
Perhaps you'd rather get to work than listen to our tune,
But come and hear us turn to song the moon's mellifluous ray,
   Diddle-diddle-boom! Derray, derray, derray.

We've seen enough of learned fools who mope alone and ponder,
While some pore on with puzzled brow, or let their wits go wander,
And some sit down in studies brown with dark and pensive faces,
Or shake their heads like silly goons and talk without a basis.
Instead of which, forget your doubts and belt out loud and gay,
   Diddle-diddle-boom! derray, derray, derray.

You slink about with haggard looks, and kill yourselves with worry,
Or waste your time by tearing round, and stumble in the scurry.
Why can't you grasp the simple truth beyond this sorry saga,
And train your feet to tap the beat that guides our noble raga?
So lift your hearts and turn your note as bravely as you may,
   Diddle-diddle-boom! Derray, derray, derray.

WAR AND PEACE

'Hullo there! Is it true you aid
The other day that white was red?
And also that last night at three
You snored completely out of key?
And even your cats all screech and howl
Like dreadful toms upon the prowl?
And none of you, the neighbours jeered,
Have learnt to grow a proper beard?
So what's all this, you stupid lout?
I'll thrash you till you're inside out.'

      'Now if just once I see you glare
      Or try my patience if you dare,
      Or once again I hear you brawl
      Like that for no excuse at all ...'

'I couldn't care two pewter pence :
I know my art of self-defence.'

      'So that's your trick? Oh well, all right,
      Come'n'fight — just come'n'fight.'

'You don't know what you're in for, mate :
You'll find out soon, but just too late.'

24

'If Uncle could be here, I know
He'd thrash you to a lump of dough.'

'Hit me, would you? You'd better stop,
Or else I'll call the nearest cop.'

'What's that? Now, now, let's not be rash :
Why don't we talk before we clash?'

'Of course — the very thing to do!
You know I'd never bully you.'

'Here, have some spice, and make an end.
My dear chap, you're my oldest friend!'

'Shake hands, old man — it's time I went.
Don't take offence where none was meant.'

'Now there's a sport! So that's all right.
It's getting late — good night, good night.'

*   *   *

Oh aunty I'm all in a fix —
    There are beans on the mulberry stalks.
The jumbos wear toadstools as wigs,
    And the jackdaws go hatching wee storks.

In Hooghly I saw only recently —
    You mustn't repeat what I've said —
Three porkers all dressed very decently,
    But none with a cap to his head.

STORY TIME

'There lived a king' — 'No, try again!
One of the king's chief serving-men.'
'His uncle, then —' 'Now heaven save you!
I'm sure it was the royal nephew.'
'He kept a goat, the poet sings —'
'A goat with such enormous wings?'
'One day upon his roof there sat —'
'A roof? You mean an iron slat.'
'The gardener who tends the plants —'
'Come, come! The man's two maiden aunts.'
'He sang a song of heroes old —'
'A hymn to spring, so I've been told.'
'Now will you let me have my say?'
'All right, all right, tell it your way.'
'When from his bed the uncle sprang,
He charged his nephew while he sang,
And grabbed his sleek hair by the root —'
'His hair? He's bald as any coot.'
'He's bald, is he? You think you know,
You niggling little so-and-so?
I'll catch you by your mingy scruff,
And baste you till you've had enough.
I'm going to make you very sorry :
You've spoilt the most exciting story.'

26

THE ENCYCLOPEDIA

This book is crammed flowing with matters of weight :
The right pecking order in bureaus of state,
The way to cook chutney or steam a pilau,
Of medical matters the wherefore and how,
The making of toothpaste, of ink and of soap,
With pujas and pundits the fit way to cope.
Just one thing seems lacking to make it quite full :
The best way to tackle a charging mad bull.

SPOOK SPORTS

The other night in moonshine bright I saw with mild surprise
A baby spook with playful look at sport before my eyes.
He laughed and sprang, and leapt and sang upon his mother's knee,
And waved his hands and burst his bands in every sort of glee.
I also caught the mother's snort of loving-pride and joy —
She grabbed his hair and swung in air her precious lively boy.
The evening breeze among the trees was rapt to hear their hooting,
Like rusty saws with iron jaws their fretful warble fluting.
She boxed his ear with loving leer and cuffed his little head
And poked his eye and tossed him high and grabbed him as he sped.
And sang to him, 'My Tiny Tim, my tatty tousled treasure,
Let's see you scowl, my pretty owl, and pout your peaky pleasure.
My podgy imp, my dancing chimp, my laughter-lapping fright,
My charming hunk, my rootling skunk in moonless woods at night,
My sunshine-thief, my summer's grief, my April shower of rain,
My sugar-pest, my syrup pressed from crunchy candy-cane,
My precious spice, my pot of rice beneath the kitchen beams,
My rider fair upon the mare of all my moonlit dreams,
My pudding-Joe, my ball of dough, my flopsy floury freak,
My crying love, my toothless dove, just let me hear one squeak ...'
She snatched a clod from off the sod to catch her child at play,
And shook her fist, and threw, and missed — and vanished quite away.

28

INFANT JOY

My God, these little fellows!
They'll go to jail, or end up on the gallows.
Here's this one daubed with flour, in frightful state —
He sits there smashing bottles with his slate.
The other crawls up cupboards to the top,
Or climbs the bed and takes a flying drop.

My God, the little devils!
They won't have milk, but want to crunch on pebbles.
One has no teeth, but licks at all he catches :
Just see him sucking candle-ends and matches.
While this one, swilling ink, is still more hellish :
He captures flies and munches them with relish.

My God, the little beasts!
Dear Uncle Tom will scarce survive such feasts.
He thinks the bread smells funny, and won't eat it,
Which makes the brats grow positively heated.
They snarl and puff : the down upon their head
Turns red with rage — poor Uncle flies in dread.

THE GRIFFON'S GROUSE

The Griffonling from birth
Is indisposed to mirth.

To laugh or grin   He counts a sin
And shudders, 'Not on earth.'

He's always in a jitter
Lest you should laugh or titter,

And peers around   At every sound
With visage grim and bitter.

Lest dignity be marred,
He's always on his guard.

'If I should splutter   Or scream,' he'll mutter,
'My! I'll catch it hard.'

* The sign reads 'Laughter Not Allowed'.

He won't go near the wood
Because he's understood

The tipsy breeze   Among the trees

May cheer his solemn mood.

And all the skyey vapours
Are merely feckless japers :

They mount the cloud   With laughter loud

In swift celestial capers.

When night begins to wake,
In every bush and brake

The dancing gleams   Of glow-worm beams

In twinkling laughter shake.

The folk whose constant diet
Is thoughtless merry riot,

How can they bear   To so impair

The Griffon's peace and quiet?

The Griffon's den lies hidden :
There cheerful thoughts are chidden,

He lines the walls   With frowns and brawls

And laughter stands forbidden.

31

GLEE SONG

O see us grin, O see us grin, a very merry threesome :
We're romping in with happy laughs, effervescent and gleesome.
Here's Brother Ned, and Brother Joe, and in between here's I :
We laugh because we want to laugh, and that's the reason why.

We sometimes wonder why we laugh, and whether we'll repent it —
But at the thought break out again, we simply can't prevent it.
It's funny when we're wide awake, it's funny when we dream,
And when we choke our sniggers back — why, that's the biggest scream.

We laugh to see a weaver's loom, an engine, ant or man,
A boat, balloon or crescent moon, an oar or oiling-can.
And when we read our ABC's, we roar without a stop :
The giggles rise from down our tums and fizz like soda pop.

THE HAND OF FATE

Dear Uncle Nanda was mild and serene,
An honest old fellow as ever was seen,
Quite hearty and hale, with his days full of grace,
A hookah in hand and a smile on his face.
But one day he went for his palm to be read,
And came back all haggard and shaking with dread.
He stared at the sky and would simply not speak,
But shuddered and moaned while the tears wet his cheek.
The people came running, the doctor ran too,
And cried, 'What's the matter? O what can we do?'
'Why, nothing,' he answered, 'My hand tells its tale :
Here Saturn rides high, and my life-line must fail.
But who could have known how my destiny lies?
Who's ever resisted the curse of the skies?
I've crossed sixty years by my forefathers' grace,
But old Uncle Nanda will soon end his race.
You simply can't tell what may happen and when ...'
And so started shaking and howling again.
I walked by his doorstep the very day after :
He'd left off his hookah, and lost all his laughter.

THE PERFUME CRISIS

The King was enthroned : they rang the great bell,
    But the Vizier sat without hope,
For the King said, 'My lord, what a very strange smell!
    Are you smearing your gown with some dope?'

'Your Majesty, sir!' cried the ancient Vizier,
    'It's simply a pleasant perfume.'
'That's easily said,' shot the King with a sneer,
    'Let the doctor examine the fume.'

But the leech wouldn't stir : 'I've a cold in my head,
    And couldn't distinguish the stuff.'
'The Chancellor, then,' His Majesty said :
    But *he'd* had a noseful of snuff.

So they hastily summoned the Chief of Police :
    He'd just chewed some betel and spices,
And what smell could last in the presence of these?
    So *he* couldn't help in the crisis.

'Why then,' said the King, 'call my First Wrestler in.'
    'I'm shaking with fever,' he swore.
'It came in the night,' he explained with a grin
    And fell fast asleep on the floor.

The King turned at last to his brother-in-law,
    Imploring his aid for the state.
'Dear boy,' he replied, 'why this devious draw?
    Why don't you just bump me off straight?'

A hoary old usher stood watching the fun —
    He must have been ninety years old.
He said to himself, 'My life's almost done :
    It really can't hurt to be bold.'

So he plucked up his courage, and 'Fiddlesticks!' cried,
    'I'm shocked at such sad hesitation.
If His Majesty asked me, I'd gladly abide —
    Of course, for a fit compensation.'

'A thousand gold pieces shall be your reward,'
    The King made his promise straight down.
The old man advanced on hearing the word,
    And lowered his nose to the gown.

He lifted its folds, he smelt every seam :
 He sniffed all the scent he could draw.
The courtroom was hushed : was it true or a dream?
 The people stood gazing with awe.

They set the bells pealing, they beat on the drum,
 The fame of the usher was rife :
A hero indeed, to do what he'd done,
 With never a thought of his life!

Clang-clang-rattle-rattle-boom-boom-tantara —
A ponderous clamour assails us from far.
The town's in uproar, and the multitudes seethe :
My Lord's infant scion is cutting his teeth.

THE GIFT OF TEARS

Those sneaky cry-babies that cry very cheaply
And yell without pondering finely or deeply,
Whine when they're hungry and weep when they're scolded,
And whimper when hurt or when suddenly jolted —
Easy laugh easy cry, stopping their chorus
At breast or at bottle or nursery stories —

I call that fake crying, a sham just to tease you :
A taste of the real stuff would stagger and freeze you.
There's Mrs. Booth's baby, next door to the Ghoshes,
Whose howls are authentic and truly atrocious.
He doesn't cry easily, stores up his grudges,
Then roars when the moment is ripe, as he judges.
A monstrous young man-child, with murderous screams
That threaten your mornings and poison your dreams.
No reason or rhyme : he pours on like a flood.
The Booths gaze appalled at the lusty young blood.
His cast-iron voice knows no break or cessation,
As roar follows roar in a gruesome succession.
He won't be enticed by the promise of treats :
You can tempt him with toys or allure him with sweets,
Or brandish a rattle, or fan him awhile,
Or dandle and stroke him — he simply won't smile.
He thrashes about with his face all a-douse,
And gapes as though straining to swallow a house.
We quake with alarm, and admit that in sooth
An infant of parts is our young Master Booth.

OLD TOM'S NOCTURNE

Creepy, lonely, silent night :
Trees stand velvet-veiled from sight.
Round the banyan's murky locks
The fireflies light their tinder-box,
And bushes hover sombrely :
Brother Tom-Cat, howl with me!
With moving mewling let's impart
The strains that melt the gentle heart.

At midnight in the eastern sky
A half-moon raised its drunken eye.
A chord awoke : last night there lay
A half-cake on the larder tray.
I ran to see on eager feet :

A crop-eared tabby clutched the sweet.
She smacked her lips with hungry zest;
All hope was snuffed within my breast.
I thought, why linger here below?
The world is but a passing show.
Our life is empty, aimless, bleared;
My mistress' face seems soot-besmeared.
O let us sing this searing pain
In wrenching verse and rasping strain.

INDIRECTIONS

Here's Jagmohan! Splendid! I'm all in a mess
In looking for Adyanath's uncle's address.
You couldn't have met him, but Khagen you know —
Well, Shyam Bagchi, Khagen's own uncle-in-law,
Has married his daughter to Kesto, you see,
Whose landlord's wife's cousin, whoever he be,
Has Adyanath's uncle as aunt's brother's son.
D'you know where he lives? For I simply must run.

Of course, my dear fellow! Just go down that street —
You know which I mean — to where three alleys meet.
Just pick one you fancy, and follow your nose,
But watch to the right and observe where it goes,
And suddenly then, where the road takes a bend,
You'll find a whole warren of lanes at the end.
Just weave through the lot, as you surely can judge,
Then sharp to the right, and then left you must trudge,
And that brings you back where the three alleys cease —
Then go where you like, only leave me in peace.

AN INVITATION

Oh don't be scared — please don't be scared! I don't intend to beat you.
Believe me, if we fought a bout, I never could defeat you.
My heart is of a kindly sort, I'm gentle in my habit —
I really couldn't crunch your neck or even try to grab it.
Perhaps it's these unfortunate horns that complicate the issue?
My forehead's in a tender state, I cannot biff or squish you.
So come and see my humble home, and take a little rest :
We wouldn't spare the slightest care to please an honoured guest.
Ah, now I know! This cudgel, then, is really why you linger?
Why bless my soul, it's light as pith, it wouldn't crack a finger!
What, still unsure? Why really, sir, you'll start to hurt my feelings :
I'll twist your neck or crush your leg to add to my appealings.
There's me, my missus, nine stout sons, the whole lot at your service —
We'll bite you all together, now, if you don't stop being nervous.

THE PURSUIT OF SCIENCE

Come here, young man, let's test your skull with my penetroscope :
What portion of your brain is dull, and what gives ground for hope.
I'll quantify the withered cells that clog your active tissues,
And defiltrate the fizzy gels from solid worthwhile issues.
Your memory is rather weak, your mind is always straying :
I'll plot the point of every leak, and chart the edges fraying.
An undulating scalp, by Gad! and also specked with mould,
And cracked as well — stand still, my lad, and do as you are told.
Twist out your tongue, and bend your neck : a biosthenic process
— Now touch your ears! — designed to check the terms of my prognosis.
A magnet to your cranium, quick! This bamboo will deflect it.
If your head reels, here comes a brick : dynamics should correct it.

THE BLIGHTY COW

A very strange bird is the Blighty Cow :
You can see him at Haru's office now.
He has dreamy eyes in a very long face,
His sleek black curls are neatly in place,
He has twice-bent horns and a corkscrew tail.
You've only to touch him — he'll scream and wail.
His legs are shaky, his joints are slack :
If you scold him, he starts and staggers right back.
No words can paint the curious creature :
This portrait limns each noble feature.
The Blighty Cow wheezes, crouched by the wall,
Or bursts out sobbing for nothing at all.
At times he's angry, and grows quite fierce,
Then falls in a fit, and gibbers and leers.
He won't eat gram or grass or hay,
Or meat or millet, wheat or whey.
He hates rice pudding and won't touch mangels :
He eats soap soup and tallow candles.
All other food sets his tum a-quiver,
He sputters and chokes, and starts to shiver.
He's had some very narrow squeaks :
He swallowed a rag and was ill twelve weeks.
If this elegant beast you'd like to buy,
I'll sell him cheaply — do apply.

HIT AND MISS

Now here's a lark, and here's a spree —
        Just roll up if you'd like to see —
Cry 'Presto' and sing 'Fiddle-dee'
        To charm the bird from off the tree
    So *pat.*

So watch this merry leap I fling,
        Then draw my bow with easy swing
And now you'll see the arrow whing
        To plug the bird beneath the wing
    Like *that.*

Here's Uncle set to field the shot :
        Just see him with his fowling-pot
Beneath the spreading branches squat —
        So now to shoot upon the dot,
    Go *crack.*

Oh curse my luck! I swerved a bit,
        The birdie saw its chance to flit,
And Uncle's in a raging fit,
        For he's the one who stopped the hit —
    Alack!

THE STRONG MAN

Our Sasti Charan, just for fun, keeps elephants to toss around :
He clocks a hundred hundredweight, his thews are truly ironbound.
They say that once a highwayman attacked him with a bamboo pole —
He lightly jut his elbow out, the bamboo snapped and down did roll.
The other day upon the street he stood beneath a falling tile —
It hit his head and smashed to smoke, while Sasti smiled a modest smile.
But why, he'd storm a mansion down if he should choose to cut up rough,
Or overturn an ox and cart with just a gentle moody puff.
He'll rip up like a paper strip the thickest knotted oaken plank,
And draw a hundred bucketfuls of water for his bathing-tank.
He breakfasts off three baskets piled with almonds, raisins, prunes and spice,
And tops this up with fourteen bowls of curds and cream with sugared rice.
His lunch is brought by teams of men in large tureens all fit to burst,
And nineteen kegs of flavoured drink are put on ice to quench his thirst.
For tea he nibbles frugally a score or two of home-made cakes,
At dinner-time a double pile of pudding-roll his hunger slakes.
At night he calls his pupils in to soothe his limbs with soft massage,
So ten young giants mount his chest and baste his limbs with cudgels large.
I really musn't tell you more, for you might think it's all a story.
Why don't you simply cross the town and view the man in all his glory?

DREAM SONG

On hazy nights, among the clouds,
Through moonlit veils and rainbow shrouds,
With crazy rhyme and puckish note
I sing my song with open throat.
There isn't any menace here,
No rule or ban or threat or fear.
Here underneath the starry beams
The breezes rock my nest of dreams,
Here leaps the spring of music-madness,
Sky-flowers toss their heads in gladness,

Light the sky and light the soul —
At every flash the wonders roll.
Today, my friend, before I go,
I'll sing you everything I know.
What if it seems to make no sense?
What if it quite confounds the dense?
My moonstruck soul I now decide
To launch upon the whimsy tide :
So who can stem my wave of song?
Or halt my thoughts that bound along?
My fancy hears, from near and far,
Trumpets sounding tantara,
And words fly up with eager bounce
All other words to trip and trounce.
The darkness lifts as moonshine wells,
Its scent adream with tinkling bells.
The heart sends out its harbingers
To greet the moonbeams' messengers.
The spirits dance in cloudy vaults
Where elephants turn somersaults

While flying steeds their wings unfold,

And naughty boys turn good as gold.
A keen primordial lunar chill,
The nightmare's nest with bunchy frill —
My drowsy brain such glimpses steep,
And all my singing ends in sleep.

A TOPSY-TURVY TALE

A translation of *Ha-Ja-Ba-Ra-La*

It was terribly hot. I lay in the shade of a tree, feeling quite limp. I had put down my handkerchief on the grass : I reached out for it to fan myself, when suddenly it called out 'Miaouw!'

Here was a pretty puzzle. I looked and found that it wasn't a handkerchief any longer. It had become a plump ginger cat with bushy whiskers, staring at me in the boldest way.

'Bother!' I said. 'My handkerchief's turned into a cat.'

'What's bothering you ?' answered the Cat. 'Now you have an egg, and then suddenly it turns into a fine quacky duck. It's happening all the time.'

I thought for a while and said, 'But what should I call you now ? You aren't really a cat, you're a handkerchief.'

'Please yourself,' he replied. 'You can call me a cat, or a handkerchief, or even a semi-colon.'

'Why a semi-colon ?' I asked.

'Can't you tell ?' said the Cat, winking and sniggering in a most irritating manner. I felt rather embarrassed, for apparently I should have known all about the semi-colon. 'Ah!' I said quickly. 'Now I see your point.'

'Of course you do,' said the Cat, pleased. 'S for semi-colon, p for handkerchief, c for cat — and that's the way to spell 'spectacles'! Simple, isn't it ?'

It didn't seem simple at all, but I nodded to stop him from sniggering again. Instead, he stared at the sky for a while and suddenly exclaimed, 'Why don't you go to Tibet if you're feeling the heat ?'

'That's easily said,' I retorted, 'but it's quite a job getting there.'

'Why, what's the problem ?' asked the Cat.

'Do you know the way ?' I asked him in return.

'Of course,' he said with a grin. 'Here's Calcutta, and here's Diamond Harbour a little to the south, and here's Ranaghat a little to the north, and then presto! you're in Tibet! Straight roads, an hour and a quarter's drive — just say the word.'

'Do show me the way,' said I.

He suddenly turned very grave, shook his head and said, 'That's beyond me,

I'm afraid. If only I had Cousin Treehopper here, he'd be able to tell you.'

'Who's Cousin Treehopper?' I asked. 'Where does he live?'

'Up in the trees, of course,' the Cat replied.

'Where can I find him?' I asked again.

'Oh, you can't do that!' he cried. 'Quite out of the question.'

'Why?' said I.

'It's like this, you see,' said the Cat. 'Suppose you're looking for him at Uluberia: you'll hear he's in Motihari. So you go to Motihari only to find he's at Ramkrishnapur. Off you go again, but they tell you there he's left for Cossimbazar. You just can't run him to earth.'

'Then how do you manage to meet him at all?' I wondered.

'It's quite a job,' said the Cat. 'First you've got to work out the places where he can't possibly be. Then you work out the places where he just possibly might; and *then* you calculate where he actually is. After that you plot where he's going to be by the time you get to where he is now. Next after that —'

I cut him short and said, 'How do you work out all these calculations?'

'It's hard work,' he replied. 'Like to see?' And he took a stick and cut a long furrow in the turf, saying, 'Suppose this is Cousin Treehopper.' Then he sat silently for a long time.

Then he cut another furrow in the same way and said, 'Suppose this is you,' and crooked his neck and fell silent again.

Then he cut yet another furrow and said, 'Suppose this is a semi-colon.' And he went on like this, pondering and drawing more and more furrows, saying things like 'Suppose this is Tibet.' ... 'Suppose this is Cousin Treehopper's wife cooking dinner.' ... 'Suppose this is a hole in the tree-trunk.' ...

After a while I felt annoyed and said, 'You're talking nonsense, and I'm getting quite bored.'

'All right, I'll make it simpler for you,' said the Cat. 'Shut your eyes and work out the sums I call out.' So I shut my eyes.

I sat like that for quite a long time without being set a single sum. In the end I got a bit suspicious and opened my eyes, only to find the Cat escaping over the garden wall with a smirk on its face.

There was nothing I could do, so I sat down again on a big stone under the tree. At once I heard a hoarse croaking voice call out, 'What's seven times two?'

I wondered what it could be this time. As I looked about me, the voice came again: 'Why aren't you answering? What's seven times two?' I looked up and saw a jungle-crow scribbling something on a slate and bobbing his head towards me.

'Seven times two is fourteen,' I answered.

He shook his head very hard and said, 'Wrong answer! No marks!'

I felt very peeved indeed. 'Of course I'm right!' I protested. 'Seven ones are seven, seven twos are fourteen, seven threes are twenty-one.'

The Crow didn't answer for a while, but just sat there sucking his pencil.

Then he began muttering, 'Seven twos are fourteen, put down four and carry the pencil.'

'Well then!' said I. 'What made you say seven twos didn't make fourteen?'

'It wasn't quite fourteen when you spoke,' answered the Crow. 'At that point it was only 13 rupees 14 annas and 3 pies. If I hadn't very cannily put down 14 just at the right moment, it would have got to be 14 rupees 1 anna and 9 pies by now.'

'I've never heard such rubbish,' I told him. 'If seven twos make fourteen, it's always fourteen, an hour ago or ten days from now.'

The Crow looked shocked and said, 'Don't you count the cost of time in your country?'

'What do you mean, the cost of time?' I asked.

'You'd know if you lived here a few days,' he replied. 'Time's terribly expensive here, we daren't waste one little bit. Here had I scraped and scrounged a bit of time together, and now I've lost half of it talking to you.' And he set to work again on his sums, while I sat by feeling rather guilty.

Just then something slithered out of a cranny in the tree and dropped to the ground. It was a little old man just three feet tall, completely bald but with a long green beard that reached down to his ankles, holding a hookah without a bowl. Somebody had scribbled on his bald head with a piece of chalk.

He took two hurried pulls at his hookah and asked very concernedly, 'Well, are the accounts ready?'

The Crow shuffled this way and that and finally said, 'Almost.'

'This is absurd,' said the Old Man. 'You've had nineteen days and they still aren't ready.'

The Crow sucked glumly at his pencil for a few minutes. Then he asked, 'How many days did you say?'

'Nineteen,' answered the Old Man.

At once the Crow called out, 'Going twenty!'

'Twenty-one!' cried the Old Man.

'Twenty-two!' cried the Crow.

49

'Twenty-three!' cried the Old Man again.

'Twenty-three and a half!' yelled the Crow, exactly as if they were bidding at an auction.

Now the Crow turned to me and frowned. 'Why aren't you bidding?' he demanded.

'Why should I?' I replied.

The Old Man hadn't noticed me all this time. Now he began spinning round and round at the sound of my voice, and finally came to a stand facing me. He then fixed his hookah to his eye like a telescope and observed me for a long time. Next he took some bits of coloured glass out of his pocket and looked at me through these. Finally he brought out an old tailor's measure and began to measure me, calling out as he did so 'Height 26 inches, arms 26 inches, cuffs 26 inches, chest 26 inches, collar 26 inches.'

'Impossible!' I said. 'How can my chest and collar both be 26 inches? I'm not a hog.'

'See for yourself,' said the Old Man.

I saw that all the figures on the tape had faded away. Only the '26' could still be made out, so everything he measured came to 26 inches.

He then asked me, 'How much do you weigh?'

'Don't know,' I replied.

He prodded me a little with two fingers and called out, '2½ seers.'

'Impossible,' I protested again. 'Patla weighs 21 seers, and I'm a year and a half older.'

'You've got a different scale of weights,' said the Crow hurriedly.

'Take this down,' the Old Man told him. 'Weight 2½ seers, age 37.'

'Of course not!' I cried. 'I'm only eight and a quarter, and I won't have you saying I'm thirty-seven!'

The Old Man considered for a moment and asked, 'Upward or downward?'

'I beg your pardon?' said I.

'Is your age increasing or decreasing?'

'How can one's age decrease?' I asked back.

'Do you mean to say it'll keep going up and up?' he exclaimed with a shudder. 'Good heavens, that way you'll end up sixty or seventy or eighty, and even grow old and die some day.'

'Of course,' I told him. 'One's very old by the time one's eighty.'

'But that's stupid!' he answered. 'Why should you ever get to be eighty? Over here, we turn our age back when we're torty. Then we don't go on to be 41 or 42, but start growing younger at 39, 38 and so on. When we've got down to ten in this way, we turn upward again. I've quite lost count how often I've grown young and old in this way. I'm thirteen now,' he added. It seemed too funny for words.

'I wish you'd talk more quietly,' said the Crow. 'I could finish my accounts that way.'

The Old Man sidled up to me at this, sat down dangling his legs, and began to whisper, 'I'll tell you a lovely story. Just let me think.' He closed his eyes and began to think his story out, scratching his bald head with his hookah all the time. Then he suddenly hissed, 'Splendid! I'm ready now'. Just listen : Meanwhile the Head Vizier had swallowed the Princess's spool of thread. Nobody knew about it. And just at this moment along came the man-eating giant, roaring as he rolled off the bed in his sleep. At once there was a hideous din of drums and bugles and cymbals and bassoons and guards and gunners and dragoons and cavalry, clash, clash, bang, bang, boom, boom, rattle, rattle — when suddenly the king cried out : 'What's this magic horse doing without a tail ?' And the pastors and masters and doctors and proctors began telling each other, 'A very good question. What's happened to its tail ?' Nobody knew the answer : they all tried to slink away.'

The Crow interrupted at this point to ask me, 'Have you got my handbill ?'

'No,' I said, so he drew out a piece of paper from a big wad and gave it to me. It said :

Corvus Sylvanus Protect Us

CROWORTHY COLE-BLACK, Esq.

Chartered Accountant

41 Raven Row, Woodmarket

We undertake all kinds of accounting work, business and unbusinesslike, wholesale and retail, on scientific principles. Rate : 1 rupee 5 annas per inch. Children half-price. For free brochure by return of post, send all relevant information such as size of shoe, colour of skin, propensity to ear-ache, whether alive or dead, etc., etc. ..

BEWARE ! BEWARE !! BEWARE !!!

We represent the reputed house of Sylvan Corvines or Jungle-Crows. It has been brought to our notice that inferior practitioners such as House-Crows, Gor-Crows and Carrion Crows are currently imposing upon the public with base profiteering intent. Do not be deceived by their vulgar publicity.

'What do you think of it ?' asked the Crow.

'I don't fully understand it,' I told him.

'Yes, it's rather difficult. Some people can't follow it at all,' he remarked. 'I once had a client with a bald head ...'

The Old Man flew into a rage. He made for the Crow, yelling, 'I won't have all this talk about bald heads, d'you hear ? Just once more and I'll crack your slate across with my hookah.'

The Crow was somewhat taken aback. He thought for a moment and said, 'I didn't say bald — I said *balled* head, meaning round like a ball.'

Even this didn't calm the Old Man, who sat muttering to himself. The Crow finally said to him, 'Want to look at the accounts ?'

The Old Man thawed a bit and said, 'Oh, have you finished ? Let me see.'

'Here you are,' said the Crow, and dropped the slate straight onto the poor man's bald head. He collapsed at once with a hand held to his head and began to howl like a baby, 'O Mummy, O Aunty, O Cousin Shiboo!' He flung his limbs about as he blubbered.

The Crow gazed at him vacantly and finally said, 'Hurt again, old chap ? I never saw such a one.'

'Two, three, four,' the Old Man began counting, stopping his tears straight away.

'Five,' cried the Crow.

I thought they were going to start bidding again, so I quickly stepped in : 'You haven't seen the accounts yet.'

'Quite so, quite so,' said the Old Man.' 'Just read what you've got there, will you ?'

I picked up the slate and found it was scrawled over closely in this way :

Be it known unto all men by these presents that whereas I Croworthy Cole-Black licensed legal practitioner accountant and notary public having considered surveyed assessed and evalued the assets fixed and unfixed movable and immovable of the principal party (hereinafter referred to as 'the party') in the case at issue hereby declare and requisition for and on behalf of the said party the right of decree right of action right of arbitration right of appeal ...

The Old Man cut me short and turned to the Crow. 'What's this drivel ?' he asked.

'You've got to write all that,' said the Crow. 'How do you expect your figures to last otherwise ? You need all that for a nice solid set of accounts.'

'Very well,' said the Old Man, 'but let's see the actual figures.'

'They're there at the end,' said the Crow; and then to me, 'Why don't you read the whole thing out ?'

I found that he'd put down in big letters at the end :

$7 \times 2 = 14$

Age : 26 inches

Cash in hand : 2½ seers

Expenditure : 37 years.

'It's obvious,' said the Crow, 'that this is neither L.C.M. nor G.C.M. So it's either Fractions or the Rule of Three. 2½ seers is a fraction, so the rest is the Rule of Three. You'd better tell me which one you'd like to have.'

'I'll have to ask,' said the Old Man. He stooped and laid his mouth to the foot of the tree, and called, 'Brother! Brother!'

After a while someone growled from inside the trunk in a huffy kind of way, 'Wha'd'you want ?'

'Croworthy wants to know something,' called the Old Man.

Again came the growl, 'What's he saying ?'

'Fractions or the Rule of Three ?' shouted the Old Man.

This time we heard quite a roar. 'Who's he calling a fraction ? You or me ?'

'No, no, he's asking whether the accounts should be in Fractions or the Rule of Three.'

After a while came the answer : 'Tell him to make it the Rule of Three.'

The Old Man gravely stroked his beard and began shaking his head. 'Just like silly old Brother! Rule of Three indeed! What's wrong with Fractions ? I really think you'd better make it Fractions, Croworthy.'

The Crow began to calculate : 'Take away two from two and a half seers and what's left is the fraction, half a seer. So your accounts come to half a seer. Half a seer of accounts costs two rupees 14 annas if it's neat, and six pice if it's mixed with water.'

The Old Man said, 'Three tear-drops fell on your figures while I was crying. So here's six pice, and here's your slate.'

The Crow seemed very pleased to get the money. He began dancing and drumming on the slate, singing 'Oh bold and brave ...'

'Did I hear you say *bald* again ?' the Old Man roared. 'Well, you've asked for it. Brother, Brother! Quick now, he's just said *bald* again.' Even as he spoke, a huge bundle of rags tumbled out of a hole in the tree. I could see an old man trapped beneath it, waving his arms and legs in an agitated manner. He looked exactly like the Old Man with the hookah. But *he*, instead of coming to his brother's help, leapt on top of the bundle instead, and sat there crying 'Get up at once, you clod,' while he beat the poor man with his hookah.

The Crow winked at me and said, 'Don't you see ? This new chap would like to pass the bundle to his brother, but he won't take it, of course. They keep quarrelling about it all the time.'

By now the old man with the bundle had managed to stand up. He lifted the bundle in a threatening way and said, clenching his teeth, 'You stupid old Other!' While Other, rolling up his sleeves, roared, 'You hateful old Brother!'

'Go on, go on,' yelled the Crow. 'Have a good fight.'

And they went at it hammer and tongs, biff, biff, thud, thud. After a minute

Other lay gasping on the ground, while Brother rubbed his bald head and shivered.

Then Brother began to bawl, 'Oh my poor, poor Other, what's happened to you?'

And Other also started howling, 'Oh my precious, precious Brother, what have I done to you?'

So they fell on each other's necks and wept for a while, then went off chatting arm in arm, as friendly as you please. Meanwhile the crow had also shut up shop and left. I was just thinking of going home myself, when I suddenly heard a strange sound in a nearby bush, as if somebody were laughing himself into stitches. I looked and found a most peculiar creature — part man, part monkey, part owl, part goblin — thrashing about with laughter and spluttering, 'It's too much — I'll burst, I know I will.'

He paused a little on seeing me, and gasped, 'Thank goodness you've come, or else I'd really have died of laughing.'

'But what makes you laugh in this monstrous way?' I asked.

'Why, it's like this,' said the creature. 'Imagine the earth were flat, and all the water in the sea were to drain onto the land, and it grew all muddy and slippery, and every one kept slipping and breaking his bones — ho, ho, ho, ho.' Again he began tumbling about with laughter.

'Surely you aren't laughing like this for such an absurd reason?' said I.

He paused again and said, 'Well, not only for that, of course. Suppose there's a man coming along, with an icecream in one hand and a lump of clay in the other, and he takes a bite out of the clay instead of the icecream — ho, ho, ho, ho.' He started laughing again.

'Why on earth,' I asked him, 'are you hurting yourself by laughing at such impossible things?'

'Oh, they aren't as impossible as you may think,' he rejoined. 'For instance, suppose there's a man who keeps lizards, and he feeds them and baths them and puts them out to dry, and along comes a billy goat and gobbles up the lot — ho, ho, ho, ho.'

He really was a most extraordinary creature. 'Who are you?' I asked him. 'What's your name?'

He thought for a while and said, 'My name's Higgle-Piggle-Dee. I'm called Higgle-Piggle-Dee, my brother's called Higgle-Piggle-Dee, my father's called Higgle-Piggle-Dee, my uncle's called Higgle-Piggle-Dee ...'

I cut him short. 'Why don't you simply say the whole family's called Higgle-Piggle-Dee ?'

He pondered the matter again. 'Oh no,' he said at last, 'I'm really called Tokai. My uncle's called Tokai, my nephew's called Tokai, my cousin's called Tokai, my father-in-law's called Tokai ...'

'Are you sure ?' I asked sternly. 'Or are you making all this up ?'

He grew quite confused and stammered, 'Well, actually my father-in-law's called Biscuit.'

This really made me very angry. 'I don't believe a word you say,' I declared.

Just then there was a rustle behind the bush, and a big bearded goat came stomping out. 'I believe you were talking about me ?' he enquired.

I was going to tell him we weren't, but he'd already launched on a long speech. 'You can argue as much as you like,' he said, 'but I tell you there are some things that goats don't eat. I would therefore like to deliver a short discourse on 'The Diet of Goats'.' He then stepped forward and began : 'Assembled children and dearly beloved Higgle-Piggle-Dee, you can see from the label round my neck that my name is Grammaticus Horner, B.A., Nutritional Consultant. I am very fond of gram, so I am known as Grammaticus, and my horns are plain to behold. I have been honoured with the degree of B.A. for my widely acclaimed skill in going ba-ba.

I have personally investigated the nature of Things That Can Be Eaten and Things That Cannot, hence my merited profession of Nutritional Consultant. I know it is proverbial to say 'Fools bleat everything, goats eat everything', but this is a foul libel. You have just heard this miserable — creature saying that goats eat lizards. This is utterly mendacious. I've had a lick at all kinds of lizards, and they simply aren't worth eating. It is true, of course, that we consume many items that

55

other species refuse — like paper bags, or coconut fibre, or newspapers, or good magazines. But we wouldn't dream of eating costly bound books. We may sometimes savour a quilt or a blanket, or perhaps a mattress or pillow, but those who accuse us of devouring beds, tables and chairs are no better than liars. When we feel inspired, the muse may induce us to face all kinds of challenges — like india-rubber, or bottle-tops, or old shoes, or canvas bags. It is reported that my grandfather chewed up half a surveyor's tent out of sheer high spirits. But of course we do not partake of knives, forks, jars or bottles. Some of us are fond of soap, but usually they are the vulgar sort with cheap tastes. And yet my own young brother once swallowed a whole bar of washing-soap ...'

At this he looked up at the sky and began to bleat in a melancholy way. Obviously his brother hadn't survived the experiment.

The Higgle-Piggle-Dee had fallen asleep, but the Goat's dreadful wailing awoke him : he sat up with a start and began to splutter and choke. I was quite afraid he'd die, but there he was again a little later, sprawling with laughter in the same old way.

'Now what's the joke ?' I asked him.

'There was once a man with a most fearful snore,' he said. 'And one stormy day there came an enormous clap of thunder, and everyone began to thrash him because they thought it was his snore ... ho, ho, ho, ho.'

'Rubbish!' I said, and was about to turn away, when I noticed a man with a smooth shaven head, wearing a collarless coat and a pair of baggy trousers, looking at me with an insufferable grin on his face. The moment he caught my eye he began to buck and simper and rub his hands, saying, 'Please, my dear fellow, don't ask me to sing right now. My voice is a little off today.'

'Here's a nuisance!' I exclaimed. 'Whoever's asked you to sing ?'

But he simply kept on whining, almost into my ear : 'Now you're getting angry. Don't tell me — I can see you're angry. Come, come, old chap, I'll sing you a few songs if you like. No need to get worked up.'

Before I could get rid of him, the Goat and the Higgle-Piggle-Dee called out together, 'Yes! Let's have a few songs!' In a twinkling, Smoothpate took out two large song-books from his pockets, held them up to his eyes, hummed a little to himself, and suddenly began to bawl, 'A rose-red song with sky-blue tune, a little scent of laughter.' He sang this single line over and over once, twice, five times, ten times.

56

'This is getting tiresome,' I told him at last. 'Don't you know any other words ?'

'I do indeed,' he replied. 'But they're out of a different song. It goes like this :

> On pavement and alley
> The revellers rally
> And paint the walls pink
> With blacking and ink.

I hardly sing this one nowadays. There's another one that begins 'O the hills where they grow new potatoes ...' You have to sing it in a Mealy and Mushy Manner. I can't manage that either these days. What I do sing quite often now is 'Peacock Plumes'. And he began at once :

> The darkness looms with peacock plumes that whisper in the welkin's ear,
> And bottle-tops with tuneful pops go sailing up so thin and clear.
> The lisping light that rambles right around the bright and tender air
> Through black and white in dreamy flight, through thick and thin goes
> floating fair.

'What kind of a song is this ?' I asked. 'I can't make head or tail of it.'

'Yes, it's awfully hard,' said the Higgle-Piggle-Dee.

'What's hard about it ?' remarked the Goat. 'Except the bit about the bottle-tops, of course.'

Smoothpate began pouting as though we'd hurt his feelings very much, and said, 'Well, if you want a simple song, you've only to say so. There's no need to make rude remarks. I'm perfectly capable of singing simple songs.' And he started off :

> The Bat said to the Porcupine, 'Old spark,
> We're going to have a proper little lark.
> The owlets and the batlings will assemble,
> The froggies and the tadpoles all a-tremble,
> The shrew will shriek, or even faint with fright :
> The wretched mouse awaits his doom tonight!'
> The Porcupine responded, 'Here's the rub :
> My missus lies asleep beneath this shrub.
> You'd better tell the Owl and all his fellows,
> If she's disturbed by screeches, croaks or bellows,
> I'll draw my quills and spank and spike and spear :
> You'd better make that absolutely clear.'
> The Bat replied, 'I couldn't in all conscience.
> The owls will simply hoot to hear your nonsense.
> The inky eve's a funny time to snore :
> Your better half's a lazybones and bore.
> And you, dear chap, are daily growing dafter :
> A soot-faced sot and batty butt of laughter ...'

I don't know how much longer he'd have gone on, but a great hubbub arose at this point. I looked about and saw quite a crowd around me. A Porcupine stepped forward and began sniffling and crying, while a Crocodile wearing a wig patted him on the back with an enormous book and whispered, 'Now don't cry, don't cry, I'll see that you have your rights.' And a large Toad in livery raised his baton and announced, 'Action for libel!'

At these words a Screech-owl in a long black gown clambered onto a big stone and fell to nodding and drowsing quite openly, while a hefty Shrew fanned him with a very dirty fan.

The Owl blinked round with his bleary eyes, fell nodding again, and mumbled, 'State the charge.'

The Crocodile now rose, puckered up his face to look as sad as possible, and poked at his eyes with his claws until he'd squeezed out a few tears. Then he began to speak in a hoarse rasping voice : 'My Lord, it behoves us to get to the root of the matter. First, then, a few words about roots. Roots are of two classes, edible and inedible. The yam is an edible root. It comes in several varieties, and is a celebrated nutriment.'

At this point a Fox, also wearing a wig, jumped up and said, 'My Lord, the yam is a toxic and execrable weed. It irritates the throat, and 'Go and eat yams' is a vulgar insult. Only pigs and porcupines consume yams.'

The Porcupine was about to sniffle again, but the Crocodile shut him up with a rap from his book and asked, 'Can you produce witnesses or documentary evidence of the charge ?'

The Porcupine pointed to Smoothpate and said, 'He's got all the documents.'

The Crocodile snatched Smoothpate's songbooks, opened one at random and began to read :
>One, two,
>What shall we do ?
>Lie on our backs,
>Tie up our packs :
>Roses in posies,
>Fishes in dishes,
>Beans and greens,
>Floors and doors,
>Wash them with soap :
>What makes you mope ?

'Not that one,' protested the Porcupine.

'Isn't it ?' said the Crocodile. 'Well, what about this ?' And he turned up another page and read :
>The moon shines bright, the witches light upon the drumstick tree
>Where mimbling schools of grubby ghouls go crackle-crunch with glee.
>The banshee swings and shakes her rings because she's feeling slighted :
>She pouts and squeaks through painted cheeks, 'I want to be invited.'
>The hairy hag, just see her wag in upsy-daisy fashion :
>She'd like a slice of soft and nice young human for her ration.

'Rubbish!' cried the Porcupine. 'You don't know what you're looking for.'
'Perhaps it's this one then?' said the Crocodile.

> Cream and curd
> Your case is heard
> A wily bird
> Just say the word —
> It's quite absurd.

'Not that one either? Well, try this —"I lie in a fright in the attic at night, and find that I'm feeling quite famished."No? What's that? A poem about Mrs. Porcupine? Why didn't you say so all this while? Here you are :

> Ram Bhajan's wife
> Is a creature of strife :
> Tossin' and pitchin'
> The pots in the kitchen,
> And thumping and sloshing
> The clothes in the washing.

Don't tell me I'm wrong! Then it's bound to be :

> My old man wheezes and coughs and sneezes, he's suffered a couple of
> strokes :

> He shudders and jibs at a crack in his ribs, it shouldn't be long till
> he croaks.

The Porcupine positively began to wail, crying, 'I'm done for! All that money down the drain! Here's a worthless lawyer for you, can't find a document when it's handed to him.'

Smoothpate had stood by all this while. He now asked, 'Which song do you mean ? "The Bat said to the Porcupine" ?'

'Yes, yes, that's the one,' said the Porcupine excitedly.

The Fox jumped up again and said, 'What *did* the Bat have to say ? My Lord, I wish to call upon the Bat as a witness.'

'First witness — Bat!' croaked the Toad.

But everybody looked around, and the Bat wasn't there at all. So the Fox went on, 'In that case, My Lord, I supplicate for the death penalty to be passed on all the accused.'

'Not on your life,' said the Crocodile. 'We're going to appeal.'

The Owl, his eyes still shut, growled, 'Appeal admitted. Summon the witnesses.'

The Crocodile glanced round warily and said to the Higgle-Piggle-Dee : 'Like to be a witness ? You'll get four annas in good money.' The Higgle-Piggle-Dee seemed only too pleased to get the money, so he jumped into the witness-box and started to giggle immediately.

'What are you giggling about ?' asked the Fox.

The Higgle-Piggle-Dee answered : 'There was once a man whom they'd coached to be a witness. They'd taught him to say that a certain book had a green cover with a blue leather spine and a blotch of red ink at the top. So when the lawyer asked him "Do you know the accused ?" he replied "Yes, your honour : he has a green cover with a blue leather spine and a blotch of red ink at the top." Ho, ho, ho, ho!'

'Do you know the Porcupine ?' said the Fox.

'Yes, your honour,' said the Higgle-Piggle-Dee. 'The Porcupine, the Crocodile, the whole pack of 'em. The Porcupine lives down a hole and has long sharp quills. The Crocodile has big bosses on his hide; he eats goats and suchlike.' At which Grammaticus Horner began to weep.

'Now what's the matter ?' I asked him.

'A crocodile chewed up half of my youngest uncle but one,' he wailed, 'and so the other half died too.'

'Well, good riddance,' I snapped. 'Now just keep quiet.'

The Fox turned again to the Higgle-Piggle-Dee. 'Do you know anything about the lawsuit ?'

'About lawsuits of all kinds,' said the Higgle-Piggle-Dee. 'There are two parties to a lawsuit. One's called the plaintiff, and he has a lawyer with him. The other's called the defendant, and he's got a lawyer too. There are ten witnesses on each side. And there's a judge who sits down and goes to sleep.'

'I haven't gone to sleep at all,' protested the Owl. 'I've got my eyes shut because there's something the matter with them.'

'Yes,' said the Higgle-Piggle-Dee, 'I've seen a lot of judges and they'd all got something the matter with their eyes, poor things.' And he began giggling again.

'What's wrong with you ?' said the Fox.

'There once was a man,' said the Higgle-Piggle-Dee, 'who had something the matter with his head, and he used to give names to things. His shoes were called Pusillanimity, his umbrella was called Perseverance, his bucket was called Plenipotentiary — but he'd no sooner named his house Paradoxicality than it fell down in an earthquake. Ho, ho, ho, ho ...'

'How interesting,' said the Fox. 'And what may you be called yourself ?'

'At present,' he replied, 'my name is Higgle-Piggle-Dee.'

'What d'you mean, at present ?' asked the Fox. 'One always has the same name, I suppose.'

'Indeed not,' said the Higgle-Piggle-Dee. 'In the morning, my name is Coconut-and-Spuds, and later in the afternoon I'll be Scarecrow Major.'

The Fox turned to the Owl and said, 'My Lord, here's a fine pack of dolts and lunatics. Their evidence has no value at all.'

The Crocodile flared up and began to lash his tail. 'Who says it has no value ?' he shouted. 'I'm buying it at four annas a time.' He made a great show of counting out the money and gave it to the Higgle-Piggle-Dee.

Someone announced from over our heads : 'Witness no. 1, price 4 annas.' I glanced up and saw Croworthy Cole-Black at his accounts again.

The Fox asked once more, 'Do you know anything else about this dispute ?'

The Higgle-Piggle-Dee thought for a while and said, 'I know a song about foxes.'

'Let's hear it,' said the Fox.

The Higgle-Piggle-Dee began to croon :

> O come and view these rousing scenes,
> Foxes wolfing aubergines.
> And all they lack by way of spoil
> A pinch of salt, a dash of oil ...

The Fox hastily stopped him, saying, 'That's about a different lot of foxes. I have no more questions to ask this witness, My Lord.'

There now began a regular stampede for the witness-box, as it seemed witnesses were being paid good money. While everybody was milling and jostling, I suddenly saw Croworthy hop down from his perch and climb straight into the witness-box. Before anyone could ask him any questions, he began : 'Corvus Sylvanus Protect Us. Croworthy Cole-Black, Esq., Chartered Accountant, 41 Raven Row, Woodmarket. We undertake all kinds of accounting work, business and unbusinesslike, wholesale and retail ...'

'Stop that rot and answer my questions,' said the Fox. 'What's your name ?'

'Croworthy Cole-Black,' said the Crow, 'I've just told you.'

'Place of residence ?'

'Woodmarket,' said the Crow. 'I've told you that as well.'

'How far away is that?' asked the Fox.

'Hard to say,' said the Crow. 'Four annas per hour, ten pice per mile, discount of two pice for cash. Ten annas by addition, three annas by subtraction, seven pice by division, twenty-one rupees by multiplication.'

'Don't show off,' said the Fox. 'Do you know your way home?'

'Of course I do,' said the Crow. 'It's the road just in front of you.'

'How far does it go?' asked the Fox.

'Why should it go anywhere?' replied the Crow. 'It stays right where it is. Roads don't roam about. They don't go for holidays in the hills.'

'You're a pretty piece of goods,' sneered the Fox. 'Do you know anything of this case in which you're supposed to be a witness?'

'I like that!' parried the Crow. 'Who's been keeping the accounts all the while, I'd like to know? Apply here for any information you need. First, there's a yam at the root of the matter. Yams belong to several species. They hurt the throats of foxes but not of crows. Next we have a witness, price 4 annas nett, whose spine used to turn black and blue. Then there was a man who gave everything names. He called the fox Oil and Grab, the crocodile Old Twister, the owl Gloomscreech ...'

At this, complete pandemonium broke out in court. The Crocodile went berserk and swallowed the Toad, the Shrew began to gibber with terror, the Fox tried to drive Croworthy out with an umbrella.

In the middle of this, the Owl started intoning: 'Silence in the court! I shall now deliver the judgment.' He turned to a rabbit with a pen stuck in his ear, and said: 'Take down what I say. Libel case no. 24. Plaintiff: Porcupine. Accused: — who *is* the accused?'

Everybody was taken aback and began saying, 'Goodness gracious! There's nobody accused!' So they quickly hustled poor Smoothpate into being the accused. The silly fellow thought the accused would also get some money, so he happily agreed. Instead he was sentenced to three months' imprisonment and seven days' hanging.

I was just thinking of protesting against such an unfair sentence, when suddenly the Goat bleated 'Gr-r-r-rammaticus!', butted me in the back, and then began to bite my ear. Next everything got a bit blurred, and the Goat came to look more and more like my uncle. When I could see plainly again, there he was, hauling me up by the ear and shouting, 'Caught you, boy! Sleeping away when you're supposed to be learning your grammar!'

I was quite taken aback. Could I have been dreaming? But honestly, when I looked round for my handkerchief, I just couldn't find it; and there on the wall sat a cat preening its whiskers, who scurried away as soon as I caught its eye. And just then a goat began bleating beyond the garden fence.

I told my uncle the whole story, but he only said, 'Nonsense, my boy. You're making up stories out of some silly dream you've had.' People turn funny as they grow old: they just don't believe things any more. But you aren't very old as yet, so I thought I'd tell you all about it.